The Little
Baking
Cookbook

THE LITTLE

BAKING

— COOKBOOK —

SMITHMARK

This edition first published in 1996 by
SMITHMARK Publishers
a division of US Media Holdings Inc.
16 East 32nd Street
New York, NY 10016

© 1996 Anness Publishing Limited

Produced by Anness Publishing Limited
1 Boundary Row
London SE1 8HP

SMITHMARK books are available for bulk purchase for sales
promotion and for premium use. For details write or call the
manager of special sales, SMITHMARK Publishers, a division
of US Media Holdings Inc., 16 East 32nd Street, New York,
NY 10016; (212 532 6600)

ISBN 0 8317 7420 7

Publisher Joanna Lorenz
Senior Cookery Editor Linda Fraser
Assistant Editor Emma Brown
Designers Patrick McLeavey & Jo Brewer
Illustrator Anna Koska
Photographers Karl Adamson, Steve Baxter,
Amanda Heywood, Michael Michaels, & Don Last
Recipes Shirley Gill, Alex Barker, Christine France,
Hilaire Walden, Patricia Lousada, Norma MacMillan,
Roz Denny, Sarah Gates & Elizabeth Wolf-Cohen

10 9 8 7 6 5 4 3 2 1

Printed in Singapore by
Star Standard Industries Pte Ltd

Contents

Introduction

At a time where so much of what we buy is pre-packed, when cookies come in rolls with tag-pulls for easy opening, freezers are filled with fudge cakes, and ready-to-fill pastry shells are on sale in every grocery store, maybe it is time to campaign for a return to home baking. Remember the smell of newly baked bread, the welcome sight of a batch of fresh scones, the taste of homemade bread packed with candied fruits? These are treats few commercial products can match, and if the demands of modern living mean we seldom have time to bake our own cookies, perhaps we need to look again at how we use the time we have. Baking is one of the most satisfying branches of cooking. Kneading dough can

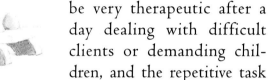

be very therapeutic after a day dealing with difficult clients or demanding children, and the repetitive task of rolling out dough, and cutting out cookies can be positively soothing as an antidote to rush hour travel. Much has been made of the dangers of a diet high in fats and sugars. When you do your own baking, you have far more control over what your family eats. Reducing the amount of refined sugar in cakes and cookies is easy to achieve, especially if you use dried fruits. Low-fat lunchbox treats, like Apricot Yogurt Cookies on page 20, are a much better bet than chocolate bars.

Home baking doesn't have to be horribly time-consuming. Bread is a cinch thanks to dried yeast, which is added directly to the dry ingredients. You can make the dough in a food processor or blender, if you choose, and as it only needs a single proving, baking a loaf of bread or a dozen rolls is simplicity itself.

Many of the cakes and quick breads in this book take very little time to produce, and even pastry, which some people regard as fiddly, is child's play if you remember these few cardinal rules: when you rub fat into flour, work fast, and lift the mixture to incorporate air; add only enough liquid to enable the ingredients to bind together; handle the dough as little as possible, and roll it out quickly and lightly. Lining pie pans, spooning in filling, and adding pastry lids can take time, especially if you crimp the edges and decorate the top of the pie, but there's no need to do any of that if you are in a hurry. Just roll out a large circle to fit the pie pan with plenty of overlap, add your filling, and place the extra pastry over. It won't cover the filling completely but that doesn't matter — the rustic effect is part of the charm. The Open Apple Pie on page 47 is made by this method, and very good it is too.

For special occasions try some of the more elaborate cakes like the Chocolate Fudge Torte on page 54 or the Raspberry & Hazelnut Meringue Cake on page 56. Either of these would make a stunning, delicious centerpiece for a celebration tea or a fitting finale to a very special dinner party.

Baking Ingredients

SUGAR

Granulated is an all-purpose sugar. Use superfine for creaming because it dissolves faster, and gives a lighter result. Brown sugar is favored for its flavor in fruit cakes.

DRIED FRUIT

An invaluable pantry ingredient, dried fruit is sold pre-cleaned and seeded for use in cakes and desserts.

NUTS

Buy nuts only when you need them if possible, as they can become rancid if kept too long. Opened packages can be stored in the fridge or freezer.

BAKING POWDER

Made from baking soda, selected acids and starch, this is an effective raising agent, and is added to flour.

BAKING SODA

This raising agent produces a rapid rise in the presence of an acid. Cakes containing baking soda should be baked as soon as possible after mixing.

FLOUR

Most of the recipes in this book use self-rising, bread or all-purpose flour. Where sifted whole wheat flour is stipulated, return the bran from the sifter to the bowl.

EGGS

Unless recipes specify otherwise, use large eggs. Keep them point-downward in their box in the fridge, allowing them to come to room temperature before use. Always buy eggs from a reputable supplier.

BUTTER

For rich cakes and pastries, butter is the fat of choice. Two types are available – sweet cream butter and lactic butter, the latter tasting slightly more acidic.

MARGARINE

For most cake mixtures, margarine gives good results. Bring block margarine to room temperature before creaming, but use soft margarine straight from the fridge.

OILS

Choose light oils with no discernible flavor for baking. Sunflower oil is ideal, but peanut oil or vegetable oil are also fine for most baking purposes.

YEAST

Breads and some cakes use yeast as the raising agent. The recent development of fast-rising yeast has revolutionized home baking because it is so quick and simple to use, although some cooks still prefer to bake with fresh yeast. A third kind of yeast, active dry yeast, has now largely been replaced by fast-rising yeast.

Baking Techniques

KNEADING

Working yeast dough by folding it toward you, then pushing it down and away with the heel of one or both hands. The dough is turned, and the action repeated, often for several minutes, until it feels elastic and no longer sticky.

FOLDING

Lightly mixing an aerated ingredient such as whisked egg whites into other ingredients so that the air does not escape. A metal spoon or a rubber spatula is used with a very light up-and-over action, turning the bowl as you work.

CREAMING

Beating together softened fats with sugar, using a wooden spoon or electric whisk, to make a mixture that resembles whipped cream.

RUBBING-IN

The diced fat (usually butter) is added to the flour, then rubbed between the fingertips until the mixture resembles breadcrumbs.

RISING

Putting the dough in a covered bowl (or the baking pan), covering, and setting aside in a warm place until doubled in bulk.

LINING A ROUND PAN

Draw two circles on wax or nonstick parchment paper to fit the bottom of the pan, and cut out. Then cut a long strip slightly longer than the circumference of the pan and about 2 inches taller. Crease the paper strip about 1 inch from a long side, then snip the paper diagonally at intervals from edge to fold. Grease the pan lightly with oil, and fit one of the paper circles in the bottom. Then fit the long strip around the inside with the snipped fringe overlapping neatly at the bottom. Brush lightly with oil, then fit the second paper circle in place at the bottom of the pan.

LINING A SQUARE PAN

Cut a piece of wax or nonstick parchment paper big enough to cover the bottom of the pan and come up the sides, adding an extra 1 inch all around. Center the pan on the paper, then make four cuts in from the side of the paper to the corners of the pan. Overlap the corners of the paper to construct a box the same shape as the pan. Grease the pan, and then fit the paper lining in place.

TIME-SAVING TIP

Freeze appropriate amounts of rubbed-in mixture. Defrost when needed, and use for cakes, pastries or crumble toppings. Add sugar and spice as required.

Cookies &
Bars

Chocolate Nut Cookies

INGREDIENTS

1 ounce semisweet chocolate, broken into squares
1 ounce bittersweet cooking chocolate,
broken into squares
2 cups flour
½ teaspoon salt
1 cup sweet butter, at room temperature
1 cup sugar
2 eggs, beaten
1 teaspoon vanilla extract
1 cup walnuts, finely chopped

MAKES 50

1 Combine the chocolate squares in a heatproof bowl. Bring a small saucepan of water to a boil, remove from the heat, and place the bowl on top. Set aside until the chocolate has completely melted, then stir until smooth. Sift the flour and salt into a small bowl, and set aside.

2 Using an electric mixer, cream the butter in a mixing bowl until soft. Add the sugar, and beat until light and fluffy. Beat in the eggs and vanilla extract, a little at a time. Then stir in the melted chocolate. Add the flour mixture and the nuts, and fold in gently until well mixed together.

13

3 Divide the mixture equally into four parts, and, with your hands, roll each into a log, about 2 inches in diameter. Wrap each of the chocolate logs tightly in

foil, and refrigerate overnight, or place the logs in the freezer for several hours until firm.

4 Preheat the oven to 375°F. Grease two or three cookie sheets. With a sharp knife, cut the logs into ¼-inch slices. Place the rounds on the cookie sheets, and bake for 10 minutes or until lightly colored. Cool on wire racks.

Florentines

INGREDIENTS

3 tablespoons sweet butter
½ cup heavy cream
½ cup sugar
1 cup sliced almonds
⅓ cup candied orange peel
¼ cup candied cherries, chopped
generous ½ cup flour, sifted
*8 ounces semisweet chocolate, broken
into squares*
1 teaspoon sunflower oil

MAKES ABOUT 36

14

1 Preheat the oven to 350°F. Grease two cookie sheets. Melt the butter, cream and sugar in a saucepan. Then bring to a boil. Remove from the heat, and mix in the sliced almonds, candied peel, cherries and flour.

2 Drop small spoonfuls of the mixture 2 inches apart on the prepared cookie sheets. Flatten with a fork. Bake for 10 minutes or until the florentines start to color at the edges. Remove from the oven, and quickly neaten the edges with a knife or round cookie cutter. Use a metal spatula to transfer the florentines to a clean, flat surface.

3 Melt the chocolate in a bowl over hot water. Add the oil, and stir until well blended. Use the spatula to spread the smooth underside of the cooked florentines

with a thin coating of melted chocolate. Arrange on a rack, and leave until almost set.

4 Draw a serrated knife across the surface of the chocolate, using a very slight sawing action, to make wavy lines. Allow to set completely before serving.

COOK'S TIP
When tidying the edges on the freshly cooked florentines, try to work fast, or they will harden on the cookie sheets. If necessary, return them to the oven for a few minutes to soften.

Chocolate-tipped Hazelnut Crescents

16

INGREDIENTS

2 cups flour
pinch of salt
1 cup sweet butter, softened
¼ cup sugar
1 tablespoon hazelnut liqueur or water
1 teaspoon vanilla extract
1 pound semisweet chocolate
½ cup roasted chopped hazelnuts
confectioner's sugar, for dusting

MAKES ABOUT 35

1 Preheat the oven to 325°F. Grease two large cookie sheets. Sift the flour and salt together into a bowl, and set aside.

2 Using an electric mixer, cream the butter in a mixing bowl. Add the sugar, and beat until fluffy. Then beat in the hazelnut liqueur or water and vanilla extract. Gently stir in the flour mixture, until just blended. Set aside 12 ounces of the chocolate, and grate the rest into the mixture. Add the chopped hazelnuts, and fold in lightly.

3 With very lightly floured hands, carefully shape the dough into about 35 2 x ½-inch crescents. Place, about 2–3 inches apart, on the cookie sheets,  then bake for 20–25 minutes until golden. Cool on the cookie sheets for 10 minutes, then use a spatula to transfer to wire racks to cool completely.

4 Line the clean cookie sheets with nonstick parchment paper. Dust the crescents with confectioner's sugar. Melt the remaining chocolate in a bowl over hot water. Using tongs, dip half of each crescent into the chocolate. Place on the prepared cookie sheets, and refrigerate until the chocolate has set.

Easter Cookies

INGREDIENTS

½ cup sweet butter or margarine
6 tablespoons sugar, plus extra
for sprinkling
1 egg, separated
1¾ cups flour
1 teaspoon ground cinnamon
⅓ cup currants
1 tablespoon chopped candied citrus peel
1–2 tablespoons milk

MAKES 16–18

1 Preheat the oven to 400°F. Lightly grease two cookie sheets. Cream the butter or margarine with the superfine sugar until light and fluffy. Then beat in the egg yolk. Sift the flour and cinnamon over the egg mixture. Then fold in with the currants and candied peel, adding enough of the milk to make a fairly soft dough.

2 Turn the dough on to a floured surface, and knead lightly until just smooth. Then roll out to a thickness of about ¼ inch. Cut into rounds, using a 2-inch fluted cookie cutter. Space the rounds on the cookie sheets, and bake for 10 minutes.

3 Beat the egg white in a small bowl. Remove the cookies from the oven, and brush them immediately with the egg white. Sprinkle them with extra sugar. Return to the oven, and bake for about 10 minutes more, until golden. Let cool on wire racks.

17

Pecan Bars

INGREDIENTS

2 cups flour
pinch of salt
½ cup sugar
½ cup sweet butter or margarine
1 egg
finely grated rind of 1 lemon
TOPPING
¾ cup sweet butter
4 tablespoons clear honey
¼ cup sugar
scant 1 cup dark brown sugar
5 tablespoons heavy cream
4 cups pecan halves

MAKES 36

1 Preheat the oven to 375°F. Lightly grease a 15½ x 10½-inch jelly roll pan. Sift the flour and salt into a mixing bowl. Stir in the sugar. Add the butter or margarine, and cut in with a knife, then rub in until the mixture resembles coarse crumbs.

2 Add the egg and lemon rind to the flour mixture, and blend with a fork until the mixture holds together. Spoon the mixture into the prepared pan, then press it out evenly. Prick all over with a fork, and refrigerate for about 10 minutes.

3 Bake the dough base for 15 minutes, then remove from the oven while you make the topping. Keep the oven on. Melt the butter, honey and both sugars in a saucepan. Bring to a boil, and boil without stirring for 2 minutes. Remove from the heat, and stir in the cream and pecan halves. Pour the mixture over the dough base, return the pan to the oven, and bake for 25 minutes more. Cool in the pan.

4 Run a knife around the edge of the dough. Invert on to a clean cookie sheet, then place another sheet on top, and invert again. Dip a sharp knife into very hot water, and cut into squares for serving.

Apricot Yogurt Cookies

INGREDIENTS

1 ½ cups flour
1 teaspoon baking powder
1 teaspoon ground cinnamon
1 cup rolled oats
½ cup light brown sugar
⅔ cup ready-to-eat dried apricots
1 tablespoon sliced hazelnuts or almonds
⅔ cup plain yogurt, plus extra yogurt or milk
(see method)
3 tablespoons sunflower oil
raw sugar, to sprinkle

MAKES 16

2 In a small bowl, whisk the yogurt and oil together. Pour into the flour mixture, and mix to a firm dough. If necessary, add a little extra yogurt or milk.

3 With floured hands, form the mixture into 16 rough mounds. Place them on the cookie sheet, leaving room for spreading, then flatten with a fork. Sprinkle with sugar, and bake for 15–20 minutes. Cool for 5 minutes, then transfer to a wire rack.

1 Preheat the oven to 375°F. Lightly grease a large cookie sheet with oil. Sift together the flour, baking powder and cinnamon into a large mixing bowl. Using a wooden spoon, stir in the oats, light brown sugar, dried apricots and nuts.

COOK'S TIP

These cookies do not keep very well, so it is best to eat them within two days, or freeze them. Pack in plastic bags, label, and freeze them for up to four months.

Quick Breads & Muffins

Apricot Nut Loaf

INGREDIENTS

2/3 cup dried apricots
1 large orange
1/2 cup raisins
2/3 cup sugar
6 tablespoons sunflower oil
2 eggs, lightly beaten
2 1/4 cups flour
2 teaspoons baking powder
1/2 teaspoon salt
1 teaspoon baking soda
1/2 cup chopped walnuts
butter, to serve

MAKES 1 LOAF

1 Line a 9 x 5-inch loaf pan with wax paper. Grease the paper well. Place the dried apricots in a bowl, and cover with warm water. Then let stand for about 30 minutes.

2 Preheat the oven to 350°F. Remove the orange rind carefully, and cut the rind into thin matchsticks. Squeeze the orange, and add water to the juice, if necessary, to make 3/4 cup liquid.

3 Drain the apricots, and cut into small pieces. Mix the orange rind, apricots and raisins in a bowl, and pour over the orange juice. Mix together well. Stir in the sugar, oil and eggs.

4 In a separate bowl, sift together the flour, baking powder, salt and the baking soda. Fold this into the apricot mixture in three batches. Stir in the walnuts.

5 Spoon the mixture into the prepared pan, and bake for 55–60 minutes or until a cake tester inserted in the loaf comes out clean. Let cool in the pan for 10 minutes, then transfer to a rack. Let cool completely before serving with butter.

Banana & Orange Loaf

INGREDIENTS

¾ cup whole wheat flour
¾ cup flour
1 teaspoon baking powder
1 teaspoon ground cinnamon
3 tablespoons sliced hazelnuts, toasted
2 large, ripe bananas
1 egg
2 tablespoons sunflower oil
2 tablespoons clear honey
finely grated rind and juice of 1 small orange
DECORATION
4 orange slices, halved
2 teaspoons confectioner's sugar

MAKES 1 LOAF

1 Preheat the oven to 350°F. Line the base of a 9 x 5-inch loaf pan with wax paper. Grease the paper with a small amount of oil. Sift the flours, baking powder and cinnamon together into a mixing bowl, adding any bran that remains in the sifter. Stir in the sliced hazelnuts. Mix until all ingredients are thoroughly combined.

2 Mash both of the bananas in a mixing bowl with a fork. Beat in the egg, sunflower oil, honey, orange rind and juice. Add to the dry ingredients, and mix well. Spoon the banana mixture into the prepared loaf pan, and smooth down the top with a knife or with the back of a spoon.

3 Bake for 40–45 minutes, or until firm and golden brown. Turn out on to a wire rack. Let cool until required. Preheat the broiler.

4 Sprinkle the orange slices with the confectioner's sugar. Place them on a rack over a broiler pan, and broil until golden, taking care not to let them burn. Cool slightly. Arrange the slices on top of the loaf.

COOK'S TIP
If you plan to keep the loaf for more than two to three days, omit the orange slices, and brush the warm loaf with honey instead. Sprinkle with sliced hazelnuts, if you like.

Sticky Gingerbread

INGREDIENTS

1 1/2 cups flour
2 teaspoons ground ginger
1/2 teaspoon ground cinnamon
1/2 teaspoon baking soda
2 tablespoons molasses
2 tablespoons light corn syrup
1/2 cup dark brown sugar
1/3 cup sweet butter
1 egg
1 tablespoon milk
1 tablespoon orange juice
2 pieces of preserved ginger, finely chopped
1/3 cup golden raisins
5 ready-to-eat dried apricots, finely chopped
3 tablespoons confectioner's sugar
2 teaspoons lemon juice

MAKES I LOAF

1 Preheat the oven to 325°F. Line a 9 x 5-inch loaf pan with wax paper. Grease the paper. Sift the flour, spices and baking soda into a mixing bowl.

2 Combine the molasses, light corn syrup, dark brown sugar and sweet butter in a heavy-based saucepan. Heat gently, stirring, until the butter has melted, and the sugar has dissolved. Take care not to overcook or the mixture will burn. Cool slightly.

3 In a small bowl, whisk the egg, milk and orange juice together. Add to the dry ingredients, together with the syrup mixture and the ginger, golden raisins and apricots. Mix well. Spoon into the prepared pan, and level the surface. Bake for 50 minutes or until the gingerbread is well risen, and a cake tester inserted in the loaf comes out clean.

4 Cool the gingerbread in the pan for 10 minutes, then remove from the pan, and cool completely on a wire rack. Beat the confectioner's sugar and lemon juice together in a small bowl until smooth. Drizzle over the top of the gingerbread, and let set. Cut into thick slices to serve.

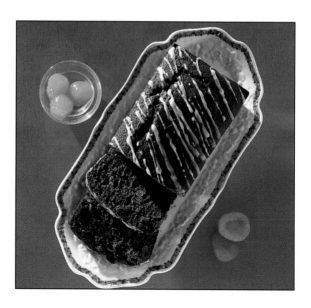

Pineapple & Apricot Loaf

INGREDIENTS

2 cups flour
¼ teaspoon salt
1½ teaspoons baking powder
¾ cup sweet butter
⅔ cup sugar
3 eggs, beaten
few drops of vanilla extract
⅔ cup crystalized pineapple, chopped
⅔ cup crystalized ginger, chopped
1⅓ cups ready-to-eat dried apricots, chopped
grated rind and juice of ½ orange
grated rind and juice of ½ lemon
milk (see method)

MAKES I LOAF

27

1 Preheat the oven to 350°F. Line a 7-inch square loaf pan with wax paper. Grease the paper. Sift the flour, salt and baking powder into a bowl.

2 Cream the butter and sugar together in a mixing bowl until pale and fluffy. Gradually add the beaten eggs, beating well after each addition, and adding a little of the flour mixture if the mixture shows signs of curdling. Beat in the vanilla extract, then fold in half of the remaining flour mixture.

3 Fold in the pineapple, ginger, apricots and grated citrus rind, with the rest of the flour. Add enough of the citrus juice to give a fairly soft dropping consis-

tency. (Add a little milk if necessary.) Spoon into the prepared pan, and level the top.

4 Bake for 20 minutes, then lower the oven temperature to 325°F, and bake for I–I¼ hours more, until firm. Cool for 10 minutes in the pan, then turn out on a wire rack to cool.

Dried Cherry Muffins

28

INGREDIENTS

1 cup plain yogurt
1 cup dried cherries
½ cup butter, at room temperature
¾ cup sugar
2 eggs
1 teaspoon vanilla extract
1¾ cups flour
2 teaspoons baking powder
1 teaspoon baking soda
pinch of salt

MAKES 16

1 In a mixing bowl, combine the yogurt and cherries. Cover, and let stand for 30 minutes.

2 Preheat the oven to 350°F. Grease a 16-cup muffin pan, or arrange 16 double paper cupcake cases on cookie sheets.

3 With an electric mixer, cream the butter and sugar together until light and fluffy.

4 Add the eggs, one at a time, beating well after each addition. Add the vanilla extract and the cherry mixture. Stir to blend, and set aside.

5 In another bowl, sift together the flour, baking powder, baking soda and salt. Carefully fold into the cherry mixture in three batches.

6 Fill the cases or muffin pan two-thirds full. Bake for about 20 minutes, until the tops spring back when touched lightly. Transfer to a wire rack to cool.

Chocolate Chip Muffins

INGREDIENTS

½ cup sweet butter or margarine
generous ¼ cup superfine sugar
2 tablespoons dark brown sugar
2 eggs, beaten
1½ cups flour
1 teaspoon baking powder
½ cup milk
1 cup semisweet chocolate chips

MAKES 10

3 Divide half the mixture between ten muffin cups or cases, and sprinkle the chocolate chips over. Then cover with the remaining mixture. Bake for 20–25 minutes, or

until the muffins are well risen. The tops of the muffins should spring back when lightly touched. If paper cases were not used, cool in the cups for 5 minutes before turning out. Serve warm or cold.

29

1 Preheat the oven to 375°F. Lightly grease a 12-cup muffin pan, or use large paper cupcake cups. With an electric mixer, beat the sweet butter or margarine with the superfine and dark brown sugar until light and fluffy. Beat in the eggs, a little at a time, adding a small amount of flour if the mixture shows any signs of curdling.

2 Sift the flour and baking powder into a separate bowl. Fold into the creamed mixture in stages, alternately with the milk.

Apple & Cranberry Muffins

INGREDIENTS

1¼ cups flour
1 teaspoon baking powder
½ teaspoon baking soda
1 teaspoon ground cinnamon
½ teaspoon grated nutmeg
½ teaspoon ground allspice
¼ teaspoon ground ginger
¼ teaspoon salt
¼ cup sweet butter or margarine
1 egg, beaten
6 tablespoons sugar
grated rind of 1 large orange
½ cup freshly squeezed orange juice
1-2 eating apples
1 cup cranberries
½ cup chopped walnuts
confectioner's sugar, for dusting

MAKES 12

30

1 Preheat the oven to 350°F. Lightly grease a 12-cup muffin pan. Sift the flour, baking powder, baking soda, ground spices and salt into a large bowl. Melt the butter or margarine.

2 Whisk together the beaten egg and melted butter or margarine. Add the sugar, orange rind and juice, and mix together well.

3 Peel, quarter, and core the apples, then chop coarsely. Make a well in the center of the dry ingredients, and pour in the egg mixture. With a large metal spoon, stir for just long enough to moisten the flour – the mixture need not be smooth.

4 Fold the apples, cranberries and walnuts into the mixture. Spoon the mixture into the muffin cups, filling them three-quarters full. Bake for 25–30 minutes until the muffins are well risen. The tops should spring back when lightly touched. Cool in the cups for 5 minutes before turning out. Serve warm or cold, dusted with confectioner's sugar.

Yeast Breads
& Rolls

Poppy Seed Knots

INGREDIENTS

1 ½ cups milk
¼ cup sweet butter
6 cups bread flour
2 teaspoons salt
¼-ounce envelope fast-rising dried yeast
1 egg yolk
1 egg, to glaze
2 teaspoons water
poppy seeds (see method)

MAKES 18

1 Heat the milk and butter in a saucepan, stirring occasionally, until the butter has melted. Pour into a pitcher, and cool to hand-hot.

2 Sift the flour and salt into a bowl. Stir in the yeast. Make a well in the center, and add the milk mixture and the egg yolk. Mix to a soft dough. Knead on a lightly floured surface for about 10 minutes, until smooth and elastic but not sticky.

3 Grease a large cookie sheet. Divide the dough into 18 pieces, about the size of golf balls. Roll each piece into a rope, and twist to form a knot. Place the knots 1 inch apart on the cookie sheet. Cover loosely, and let rise in a warm place until the knots have doubled in size.

4 Preheat the oven to 450°F. Beat the egg with the water in a cup. Brush the glaze over the knots, and sprinkle with the poppy seeds. Bake for 12–15 minutes or

until the tops of the knots are lightly browned. Transfer the knots to a rack, and let cool slightly before serving warm.

Clover Leaf Rolls

INGREDIENTS

1¼ cups milk
¼ cup sweet butter
4–5 cups bread flour
2 teaspoons salt
2 tablespoons sugar
¼-ounce envelope fast-rising dried yeast
1 egg, beaten
melted butter, for glazing

MAKES 24

34

1 Place the milk and butter in a saucepan, and heat, stirring occasionally, until the butter has melted. Pour into a pitcher, and cool to hand-hot.

2 Sift 4 cups of the bread flour with the salt into a large bowl. Stir in the sugar and yeast. Make a well in the center, and add the milk and butter mixture. Then add the beaten egg. Mix to a rough dough, adding more flour if necessary. Knead on a lightly floured surface for about 10 minutes, until the dough is smooth, elastic and no longer sticky.

3 Grease two 12-cup muffin pans with a small amount of oil. Divide the dough into four equal pieces, and, with your hands, roll each piece to a

rope about 14 inches long. Cut each rope into 18 pieces, and form each piece into a small ball.

4 Place three of the balls, side by side, in each muffin cup. Cover loosely, and let rise in a warm place until it has almost doubled in size. Meanwhile, pre-

heat the oven to 450°F. Brush the rolls lightly with melted butter to glaze. Bake for about 12–15 minutes or until lightly browned. Cool slightly on a wire rack before serving.

Multi-grain Bread

INGREDIENTS

generous ¾ cup rolled oats
2½ cups milk
4 tablespoons sunflower oil
⅓ cup light brown sugar
2 tablespoons clear honey
4 cups bread flour
2 cups soy flour
3 cups whole wheat flour
½ cup wheat germ
2 teaspoons salt
2 x ¼-ounce envelopes fast-rising dried yeast
2 eggs, lightly beaten

MAKES 2 LOAVES

1 Place the oats in a large bowl. In a saucepan, bring the milk to just below boiling point. Pour the hot milk over the oats, then stir in the oil, sugar and honey.

2 Allow the oat mixture to cool. Combine all of the flours, and the wheat germ, salt and yeast in a large mixing bowl. Add the oat mixture and eggs, and mix to a rough dough. Knead on a lightly floured surface for about 10 minutes, until smooth and elastic.

3 Grease two 9 x 5-inch loaf pans. Divide the dough into four equal pieces, and roll each to a cylinder slightly longer than the pan and 1½ inches thick. Twist the cylinders together in pairs, and place in the pans. Cover loosely, and let rise in a warm place until doubled in size.

4 Preheat the oven to 425°F. Bake the loaves for about 30–35 minutes, or until the bottom of each of the loaves sounds hollow when it is lightly tapped. (Tap the bottom of both of the loaves by clenching your hand together to make a fist, and hold the top of the loaf with your other hand.) Cool on a rack.

Danish Wreath

INGREDIENTS

¾ cup milk
4 cups bread flour
½ teaspoon salt
¼ cup sugar
¼-ounce envelope fast-rising dried yeast
½ teaspoon vanilla extract
1 egg, beaten
2 x 4-ounce blocks of sweet butter
1 egg yolk
2 teaspoons water
chopped pecans or walnuts, for sprinkling
FILLING
generous 1 cup dark brown sugar
1 teaspoon ground cinnamon
½ cup pecans or walnuts, toasted and chopped
ICING
¾ cup confectioner's sugar
a little water

SERVES 10–12

1 Heat the milk until hand-hot. Sift the flour and salt into a bowl. Stir in the sugar and yeast. Make a well, and add the milk, vanilla extract and egg. Mix to a rough dough. Knead on a lightly floured surface for 10 minutes, until smooth and elastic. Wrap, and refrigerate for 15 minutes.

2 Place each block of butter between two sheets of wax paper. Flatten each one with a rolling pin to a 6 x 4-inch rectangle.

3 Roll out the dough to a 12 x 8-inch rectangle. Place one butter rectangle in the center, and fold the bottom third of dough over. Seal the edge. Place the second butter rectangle on top, and cover with the top third of the dough. Roll out to the original size, and fold into thirds. Wrap in plastic film, and refrigerate for 30 minutes.

4 Repeat the rolling, folding and refrigerating twice more. Then refrigerate for 1–2 hours. Stir the filling ingredients together.

5 Grease a cookie sheet. Roll out the dough to a 25 x 6-inch strip. Spread the filling over it, leaving a ½-inch border. Roll up lengthwise into a cylinder. Form this into a circle on the cookie sheet, pinching the edges together to seal firmly. Cover, and let rise for 45 minutes.

6 Preheat the oven to 400°F. Slash the top of the wreath with a knife, at regular intervals. Beat together the egg yolk and water, and brush over the wreath. Bake the wreath for 35–40 minutes. Cool on a wire rack. Meanwhile, make a thin icing by mixing the confectioner's sugar with a little water. When the wreath is cold, decorate it by spooning over the icing. Sprinkle with the chopped nuts.

Cinnamon & Walnut Yeast Cake

INGREDIENTS

8 cups bread flour
2 teaspoons salt
¼ cup sugar
2 tablespoons fast-rising dried yeast
1½ cups milk
½ cup water
generous ¾ cup sweet butter
2 eggs, beaten
1½ teaspoons grated orange rind
1¼ cups confectioner's sugar
3-4 tablespoons orange juice
FILLING
scant ½ cup superfine sugar
½ cup walnuts, finely chopped
1½ teaspoons ground cinnamon

MAKES 2 CAKES

1 Sift the flour and salt into a large bowl. Stir in the sugar and yeast. Heat the milk and water with half the butter in a saucepan until the butter has melted. Pour into a pitcher, and cool to hand-hot.

2 Make a well in the center of the dry ingredients, and add the eggs, grated orange rind and the milk mixture. Mix, gradually incorporating the surrounding flour, to make a soft dough. If necessary, add a little more flour.

3 Knead the dough on a lightly floured surface for about 10 minutes, until it is smooth, elastic and no longer sticky.

4 Mix the filling ingredients in a bowl. Grease two 10-inch round cake pans. Knead the dough lightly, and divide it in half. On a lightly floured surface, roll out one piece to a 12 x 8-inch rectangle. Melt the remaining butter. Brush half the butter over the dough, and set the rest aside. Sprinkle over half the filling, and roll up tightly from a long side. Pinch the seam to seal it.

5 With a sharp knife, cut the roll across in 1-inch slices. Arrange the slices, cut side down, in the prepared pans. Repeat the process with the rest of the  dough, melted butter and filling. Cover both pans, and leave the dough to rise in a warm place until the dough slices have almost doubled in size. Preheat the oven to 375°F.

6 Bake the cakes for about 30–35 minutes or until golden. Cool on a rack. Decorate by mixing the confectioner's sugar with enough orange juice to make a thin icing. Drizzle over the cakes. Let set.

Pies & Tarts

Walnut & Pear Lattice Pie

INGREDIENTS

2 cups flour
¼ teaspoon salt
½ cup refrigerated butter, diced
¼ cup finely chopped walnuts
3-4 tablespoons iced water
⅓ cup confectioner's sugar
1 tablespoon lemon juice
FILLING
2 pounds pears
¼ cup sugar
4 tablespoons flour
½ teaspoon grated lemon rind
3 tablespoons raisins or golden raisins
3 tablespoons chopped walnuts
½ teaspoon ground cinnamon

SERVES 6–8

1 Sift the flour and salt together into a mixing bowl. Rub in the butter, and stir in the walnuts and enough iced water to moisten. Gather into a ball, wrap, and refrigerate for 30 minutes. Preheat the oven to 375°F.

2 Make the filling. Peel the pears, and slice into a bowl. Add the sugar, flour and rind. Toss to coat the fruit. Add the raisins or golden raisins, walnuts and cinnamon. Mix lightly.

3 Roll out half the pastry on a lightly floured surface, and line a 9-inch pie plate that is 2 inches deep. Roll out the remaining pastry to an 11-inch round, and cut it into ½-inch wide strips. Spoon the filling into the pastry shell. Arrange the pastry strips on top, carefully weaving them in and out to make a lattice. Bake for 55 minutes or until golden.

4 Combine the confectioner's sugar, lemon juice and 1–2 teaspoons water in a bowl. Mix until smooth. Remove the pie from the oven, and drizzle the confectioner's sugar glaze over the top. Then let cool to lukewarm before serving.

43

Red Berry Tart with Lemon Cream Filling

INGREDIENTS

1 ¼ cups flour
¼ cup cornstarch
3 tablespoons confectioner's sugar
scant ½ cup refrigerated sweet butter, diced
2 egg yolks
1 teaspoon vanilla extract
sprig of mint, to decorate

FILLING

scant 1 cup cream cheese, softened
3 tablespoons lemon curd
grated rind and juice of 1 lemon
confectioner's sugar (see method)
2 cups mixed red berry fruits
3 tablespoons red currant jelly

SERVES 6–8

1 Sift the flour, cornstarch and sugar into a bowl. Rub in the butter until the mixture resembles breadcrumbs. (This can be done in a food processor). Beat the egg yolks with the vanilla extract in a cup. Add to the dry ingredients, and mix to a firm dough, adding a little cold water if necessary.

2 Roll the pastry out into a round, and use to line a 9-inch pie pan, pressing the pastry well up the sides after trimming. Prick the pastry shell all over with  a fork. Refrigerate for 30 minutes. Line the pastry shell with wax paper, and fill with baking beans.

3 Preheat the oven to 400°F. Place the pastry shell on a cookie sheet, and bake for 20 minutes, removing the paper and beans for the last 5 minutes. Cool, then remove the pastry shell from the pan, and place on a serving plate.

4 Cream together the cheese, lemon curd, lemon rind and lemon juice, adding some confectioner's sugar to sweeten, if desired. Spread the mixture in the pastry  shell, and then arrange the mixed berries on top. Warm the red currant jelly in a saucepan, and strain it. Trickle or brush it over the fruit. Decorate the tart with a sprig of mint, and serve at once.

Plum Pie

INGREDIENTS

2½ cups flour
1 teaspoon salt
⅓ cup refrigerated sweet butter
½ cup refrigerated shortening
4-8 tablespoons iced water
milk, for glazing
FILLING
2 pounds red or purple plums, halved and pitted
grated rind of 1 lemon
1 tablespoon lemon juice
½-¾ cup sugar
3 tablespoons quick-cooking tapioca
pinch of salt
½ teaspoon ground cinnamon
¼ teaspoon grated nutmeg

SERVES 8

1 Sift the flour and salt into a bowl. Rub in the butter and shortening until the mixture resembles breadcrumbs. Stir in just enough iced water to bind the pastry. Gather into two balls, one slightly larger than the other. Wrap, and refrigerate for 20 minutes.

2 Preheat the oven to 425°F. Line a cookie sheet with wax paper. Set it aside. Roll out the larger piece of pastry to a thickness of about ⅛ inch, and line a 9-inch pie pan.

3 Roll out the smaller piece of pastry to a round slightly larger than the top of the pie. Support it on the prepared cookie sheet, then stamp out four hearts from the center of the pastry, using a cutter. Reserve the pastry hearts.

4 Make the filling by mixing all the ingredients in a bowl. Use the larger quantity of sugar if the plums are very tart. Spoon the filling into the pastry shell, then lift the pastry on the wax paper, and slide it into position over the filling. Trim, and pinch to seal. Arrange the cut-out pastry hearts on top. Glaze the top of the pie with milk, and bake for 15 minutes. Lower the oven temperature to 350°F, and bake for 30–35 minutes more, protecting the top with foil if needed.

46

Open Apple Pie

INGREDIENTS

2½ cups flour
½ teaspoon salt
½ cup refrigerated sweet butter, diced
¼ cup refrigerated shortening, diced
5-6 tablespoons iced water
FILLING
3 pounds sweet-tart firm eating or
cooking apples
¼ cup sugar
2 teaspoons ground cinnamon
grated rind and juice of 1 lemon
2 tablespoons butter, diced
2-3 tablespoons clear honey

SERVES 8

1 Sift the flour and salt together into a mixing bowl. Rub in the butter and shortening until the mixture resembles coarse breadcrumbs. Stir in just enough iced water to moisten the dry ingredients, then gather together to make a ball. Wrap the pastry, and refrigerate for 30 minutes.

2 Preheat the oven to 400°F. Very lightly grease a deep 9-inch pie pan, and set aside. Peel, quarter and core the apples, then slice them into a bowl. Add the sugar, cinnamon, lemon rind and juice, and toss them together well.

3 Roll out the pastry on a lightly floured surface to a 12-inch round. Place the pastry over the pie pan so that the excess dough overhangs the edges. Fill with the apple mixture. Then fold in the pastry edges, crimping them loosely to make a decorative border. Dot the apples with the diced butter.

4 Bake the pie for about 45 minutes, until the pastry is golden, and the apples are tender. Melt the honey in a saucepan. Remove the pie from the oven, and immediately brush the honey over the apples to glaze. Serve warm or at room temperature.

47

Mince Pies

INGREDIENTS

4 cups flour
1 cup confectioner's sugar
1½ cups refrigerated sweet butter, diced
grated rind and juice of 1 orange
milk, for glazing
confectioner's sugar, for dusting
FILLING
¾ cup blanched almonds, very finely chopped
scant 1 cup dried apricots, finely chopped
1 cup raisins
scant 1 cup currants
scant 1 cup candied cherries
scant 1 cup chopped candied citrus peel
¾ cup suet
grated rind and juice of 2 lemons
grated rind and juice of 1 orange
generous 1 cup dark brown sugar
4 cooking apples
2 teaspoons ground cinnamon
1 teaspoon grated nutmeg
½ teaspoon ground cloves
1 cup brandy
1 cup cream cheese
2 tablespoons superfine sugar

MAKES 36

1 Make the filling. Mix the nuts, dried and preserved fruit, suet, citrus rind and juice and brown sugar in a large bowl. Quarter, core, and peel the apples. Chop them finely or grate them, and add them to the bowl with the spices. Stir in the brandy. Cover the mincemeat, and set aside in a cool place for a couple of days.

2 For the pastry, sift the flour and confectioner's sugar into a bowl. Rub in the butter until the mixture resembles breadcrumbs. Add the orange rind. Stir in enough orange juice to moisten, then gather into a ball. Wrap, and refrigerate for 30 minutes.

3 Preheat the oven to 450°F. Beat together the cream cheese and superfine sugar. Roll out just over half the pastry on a lightly floured surface to a thickness of ⅛ inch. Using a 3-inch fluted cutter, stamp out 36 rounds. Fit the rounds in muffin cups. Half fill each with mincemeat, and top with about 1 teaspoon of the cream cheese mixture.

4 Roll out the remaining pastry, and use a 2-inch cutter to stamp out 36 lids. Brush the edges of the filled pastry shells with milk, then set the rounds on top. Cut a small steam vent in the top of each.

5 Glaze the pies lightly with milk. Bake for 15–20 minutes, until golden. Cool for 10 minutes before easing out on to a wire rack. Serve warm or at room temperature, dusted with confectioner's sugar.

Iced Strawberry Pie

INGREDIENTS

2 cups graham cracker crumbs
1 tablespoon sugar
5 tablespoons sweet butter, melted
1 cup cream cheese, softened
1 cup sour cream
5 cups strawberries, defrost if frozen

SERVES 8

50

1 Make the base by mixing the cracker crumbs and sugar with the melted butter in a bowl, stirring well to combine. Press the crumb mixture evenly over the bottom and sides of a 9-inch pie pan, then freeze until the crumb shell is firm.

2 Beat the cream cheese in a bowl with a wooden spoon. Gradually add the sour cream, beating the mixture until it is smooth. Slice the strawberries. Set aside a quarter of them for the topping, and fold the rest into the mixture. Pour the filling into the crumb shell, and freeze for 6–8 hours until firm.

3 To serve, cut the iced pie into slices, and spoon over some of the reserved strawberries, with a little of their juice.

Chocolate Cheesecake Pie

INGREDIENTS

1 1/2 cups cream cheese, softened
4 tablespoons heavy cream
1 cup sugar
1/2 cup cocoa powder
1/2 teaspoon ground cinnamon
3 eggs
BASE
1 1/2 cups graham cracker crumbs
8 amaretti cookies, crushed
(or extra graham cracker crumbs)
1/3 cup sweet butter, melted
DECORATION
whipped cream
chocolate curls

SERVES 8

1 Preheat the oven to 350°F. Make the base by mixing the crushed cookies with the melted butter. Press the mixture evenly over the bottom and sides of a 9-inch pie pan. Bake for 8 minutes, then let cool. Leave the oven on, and put a cookie sheet inside so that it heats up.

2 Beat the cheese and cream in a bowl with an electric mixer until smooth. Beat in the sugar, cocoa and cinnamon until blended. Then add the eggs, one at a  time, beating for just long enough to combine. Pour the filling into the crumb shell, and bake on the hot cookie sheet for 25–30 minutes. The filling will sink as the cheesecake cools. Decorate with whipped cream and chocolate curls when cold.

51

Cakes & Tortes

American Carrot Cake

INGREDIENTS

1 cup sunflower oil
¾ cup sugar
3 eggs
1½ cups flour
1½ teaspoons baking powder
1½ teaspoons baking soda
¼ teaspoon salt
1½ teaspoons ground cinnamon
¼ teaspoon grated nutmeg
¼ teaspoon ground ginger
1 cup chopped walnuts
2 large carrots, finely grated
1 teaspoon vanilla extract
2 tablespoons sour cream
8 tiny marzipan carrots, to decorate
FROSTING
¾ cup whole cream cheese
2 tablespoons sweet butter, softened
2 cups confectioner's sugar

SERVES 8

1 Preheat the oven to 350°F. Base-line, and grease two 8-inch cake pans. Beat the oil and sugar together, and add the eggs, one at a time, beating well after each addition. Sift the flour, baking powder, baking soda, salt and spices into the bowl. Beat well, then stir in the chopped walnuts, carrots, vanilla extract and sour cream.

2 Divide the mixture between the prepared pans. Bake for 40–50 minutes or until well risen and springy to the touch. Cool the cake layers in their pans on a wire rack.

3 Meanwhile make the frosting. Beat together the cream cheese, butter and confectioner's sugar, using a wooden spoon, until smooth.

4 Sandwich the cake layers together with a little of the frosting. Spread the rest over the top and sides of the cake, using a round-bladed knife to make a swirling pattern. Decorate the cake with the tiny marzipan carrots just before serving.

53

Chocolate Fudge Torte

INGREDIENTS

8 ounces bittersweet chocolate, chopped
1/2 cup sweet butter, diced
2/3 cup water
1 cup sugar
2 teaspoons vanilla extract
2 eggs, separated
2/3 cup sour cream
2 1/2 cups flour
2 teaspoons baking powder
1 teaspoon baking soda
pinch of cream of tartar
chocolate curls, raspberries and confectioner's
sugar, to decorate
CHOCOLATE FUDGE FILLING
1 pound bittersweet chocolate, chopped
1 cup sweet butter
5 tablespoons brandy
3/4 cup seedless raspberry preserve
GANACHE
1 cup heavy cream
8 ounces bittersweet chocolate, chopped
2 tablespoons brandy

SERVES 18–20

1 Preheat the oven to 350°F. Base-line, and grease a 10-inch springform pan. Place the chocolate, sweet butter and water in a pan. Heat gently, until melted.

2 Pour into a large bowl, and beat in the sugar and vanilla extract. Let cool, then beat in the egg yolks. Fold in the sour cream. Sift the dry ingredients, then fold them into the mixture. Whisk the egg whites in a bowl until stiff, and gently fold in.

3 Pour the mixture into the pan. Bake for 45–50 minutes. Let cool for 10 minutes, then remove from the pan. Let cool completely on a wire rack.

4 Make the fudge filling. Gently melt the chocolate and butter with 4 tablespoons of brandy. Set aside to cool. Meanwhile, cut the cake into three layers. Heat the preserve with the remaining brandy, and spread over each cake layer. Let set.

5 Return the bottom layer to the pan, and spread with half the filling. Top with the middle cake layer. Spread over the remaining filling, add the top cake layer, and press down gently. Refrigerate overnight.

6 Make the ganache. Bring the cream to a boil, remove from the heat, and stir in the chocolate, then the brandy. Strain, then set aside for 5 minutes to thicken. Remove the cake from its pan. Pour the ganache over the top, and cover the sides. Pipe any remaining ganache around the base of the cake using a star-shape nozzle. When set, decorate with chocolate curls, raspberries and confectioner's sugar. Do not refrigerate the glazed cake.

54

Raspberry & Hazelnut Meringue Cake

INGREDIENTS

4 egg whites
1 cup superfine sugar
few drops of vanilla extract
1 teaspoon malt vinegar
1 cup roasted chopped hazelnuts, ground
1¼ cups heavy cream
3 cups raspberries
confectioner's sugar, for dusting
mint sprigs, to decorate
SAUCE
2 cups raspberries
3-4 tablespoons confectioner's sugar
1 tablespoon orange liqueur

SERVES 6

1 Preheat the oven to 350°F. Baseline, and grease two 8-inch cake pans. Whisk the egg whites in a large bowl until stiff peaks form. Gradually whisk in the superfine sugar. When stiff, gently fold in the vanilla, vinegar and nuts.

2 Divide the mixture between the pans, and bake for 50–60 minutes, or until they are crisp. Remove gently from the pans, and let cool on a wire rack.

3 Make the sauce. Purée the raspberries with the confectioner's sugar and liqueur in a food processor or blender. Press through a fine strainer into a pitcher. Refrigerate until ready to serve.

4 In a bowl, whip the cream to soft peaks. Gently fold in the raspberries. Place one round of meringue on a serving plate, and spread the raspberry and cream

mixture evenly over the top. Place the second round of meringue on top to form a sandwich.

5 Dust the top of the cake liberally with confectioner's sugar, and decorate with mint sprigs. Serve with the raspberry sauce. To cut the cake, use a large and very sharp knife.

56

Chocolate Cream Cake

INGREDIENTS

¾ cup soft margarine
½ cup sugar
4 tablespoons light corn syrup
1½ cups self-rising flour, sifted
3 tablespoons cocoa powder, sifted
½ teaspoon salt
3 eggs, beaten
1-2 tablespoons milk (optional)
⅔ cup whipping cream
1-2 tablespoons fine-shred marmalade
confectioner's sugar, for dusting

SERVES 8–10

1 Preheat the oven to 350°F. Base-line, and grease two 7-inch cake pans. Combine the margarine, sugar, corn syrup, flour, cocoa, salt and eggs in a large bowl and beat until smooth. Alternatively use a food processor fitted with a plastic blade, using the slowest speed. Beat in enough milk to give a soft dropping consistency. Divide the mixture between the pans and spread evenly.

2 Bake the cake layers for 30 minutes or until the tops are just firm, and the cakes are springy to the touch. Cool in the pans for 5 minutes, then invert the cake layers on wire racks to cool completely.

3 Whip the cream in a bowl until it holds soft peaks, then gently fold in the marmalade. Reserving the best cake layer for the top, sandwich the layers together with the flavored cream. Dust the cake with confectioner's sugar, and transfer to a serving plate.

Blueberry Cupcakes

INGREDIENTS

½ cup soft margarine
½ cup sugar
1 teaspoon grated lemon rind
2 eggs, beaten
1 cup self-rising flour, sifted
pinch of salt
½ cup whipping cream
¾–1 cup blueberries
confectioner's sugar, for dusting

MAKES 12–14

1 Preheat the oven to 375°F. Grease a 12-cup muffin pan or arrange 12–14 paper cupcake cases on cookie sheets.

2 Cream together the margarine and sugar in a large bowl until pale and fluffy, then stir in the lemon rind. Beat in the eggs, a little at a time, then fold in the flour and salt, until well mixed. Divide the mixture between the muffin pan or cupcake cases. Bake for 15–20 minutes, until golden. Cool on a wire rack.

3 Using a sharp-pointed, small knife, carefully cut out a circle of sponge from the top of each cake. Set these sponge circles aside until required.

4 Whip the cream in a bowl. Place a spoonful of cream on each cupcake. Add two or three blueberries, and replace the sponge lids at an angle. Sift confectioner's sugar over the top of each cupcake.

Orange & Apricot Roulade

INGREDIENTS

4 egg whites
½ cup raw superfine sugar
½ cup flour
finely grated rind of 1 small orange
3 tablespoons orange juice
confectioner's sugar, for dusting
shreds of orange rind, to decorate
FILLING
⅔ cup ready-to-eat dried apricots
⅔ cup orange juice

SERVES 6

1 Preheat the oven to 400°F. Grease a 13 x 9-inch jelly roll pan, and line it with a piece of nonstick parchment paper. Grease the paper well. Whisk the egg whites in a grease-free bowl until soft peaks form. Gradually add the superfine sugar, whisking hard after each addition, then gently fold in the flour, orange rind and juice.

2 Spoon the mixture into the prepared jelly roll pan, and spread it evenly. Bake for 15–18 minutes, or until the sponge is firm and pale golden in color.

Turn out on to a sheet of nonstick parchment paper. Working quickly, roll up the sponge loosely from one short side, and let cool.

3 Make the filling. Coarsely chop the apricots, and place them in a saucepan with the orange juice. Bring to simmering point, cover, and cook until most of the liquid has been absorbed. Purée the apricots in a food processor or blender. Cool.

4 Carefully unroll the roulade, and spread evenly with the apricot purée. Roll up again, and transfer to a platter. Arrange paper strips diagonally across the roll.

Sprinkle it lightly with confectioner's sugar, then carefully remove the paper to create the patterned effect. Decorate with orange rind, and serve.

White Chocolate & Strawberry Torte

INGREDIENTS

4 ounces fine quality white chocolate, chopped
1/2 cup heavy cream
1/2 cup milk
1 tablespoon rum or vanilla extract
1/2 cup sweet butter, softened
3/4 cup superfine sugar
3 eggs
2 cups flour
1 teaspoon baking powder
pinch of salt
6 cups strawberries, sliced,
plus extra for decorating
3 cups whipping cream
2 tablespoons rum
WHITE CHOCOLATE MOUSSE FILLING
9 ounces fine quality white chocolate, chopped
1 1/2 cups whipping or heavy cream
2 tablespoons rum

SERVES 10

1 Preheat the oven to 350°F. Grease, and flour two 9-inch round cake pans, about 2 inches deep. Baseline the pans with nonstick parchment paper. Melt the chocolate in the cream in a double boiler over low heat, stirring until smooth. Stir in the milk and rum or vanilla extract. Set aside to cool.

2 Cream the butter and sugar until fluffy. Beat in the eggs one at a time. Sift together the flour, baking powder and salt. Stir into the egg mixture in batches, alternately with the melted chocolate, until just blended.

3 Divide the mixture between the pans. Bake for 20–25 minutes or until a cake tester inserted in the center of each cake layer comes out clean. Cool in the pans for 10 minutes. Turn out on to wire racks, peel off the parchment paper, and let cool.

4 Make the filling. Melt the chocolate with the cream in a saucepan over low heat, stirring frequently. Stir in the rum, and pour into a bowl. Refrigerate until just set, then whip the mixture lightly until it has a mousse-like consistency.

5 Slice each cake layer in half horizontally to make four layers. Spread a third of the mousse on top of one layer, and arrange a third of the strawberries over the mousse. Place another cake layer on top of the first, and cover with mousse and strawberries as before. Repeat this process once more, then top with the final cake layer.

6 Whip the cream with the rum. Spread about half the flavored cream over the top and sides of the cake. Use the remaining cream and strawberries to decorate the cake.

Index